Sir Jame

(

London, SW8 4JB

When I Lived
Down Cuckoo Lane...

Andersen Young Readers' Library

—— JEAN WILLS ——

When I Lived
Down Cuckoo Lane...

ILLUSTRATED BY MARY REES

Andersen Press · London

First published in 1988 by
Andersen Press Limited,
62-65 Chandos Place, London WC2

British Library Cataloguing in Publication Data
Wills, Jean
When I lived down cuckoo lane—
I. Title II. Rees, Mary
823'.914 J PZ7
ISBN 0-86264-194-2

Printed and bound in Great Britain
by Anchor Brendon Limited, Tiptree, Essex
Typesetting by Print Origination (NW) Ltd., Formby, Liverpool

Contents

To my best friend

I

. . . and Arrived in a Blizzard

'Trust us,' Mum said, 'to move out of town on a day like this.'

Outside it was snowing. There was a big van in the road. Big men clumping up and down the stairs to our flat. When all the furniture had gone, 'See you down Cuckoo Lane,' they said.

As the van moved off we went to the station and caught the tube. Mum, Dad, me and Charlie.

What would out of town be like?

When the train came up from under the ground I saw buildings with white coats. Wet black roads like pencil marks. Mushroom trees and here and there, packs of little houses.

Would ours be like one of those?

After the doors had slid open three times more we stepped out on to the platform of Greenfields Station.

Outside the station we caught a Number 55

bus. I sat up behind the driver. He had a big hunched back and wore a red woolly scarf. The tips of his ears were red to match.

It was so cold in the bus we could see our breath. Except for Charlie, who was a woolly rabbit and didn't have any.

I rubbed a clear patch on my window. The snow seemed different out of town. Thicker. Whiter.

Then Dad tapped me on the shoulder.

'Time to go.'

As we stepped off the bus the snow came at us, tingly and soft.

'Trust us,' Mum said, 'to arrive in a blizzard.'

There was the name up on the wall. Cuckoo Lane. A new white road, with new white houses. We'd never lived in a house before. Mum, Dad, me and Charlie.

'Which house is ours?'

'The last one, on the right-hand side. Number 54,' Dad said.

The removal men had beaten us. Their van sat outside our house. Beyond was a long white empty slope. An empty stretch. Then distant

blobs of mushroom trees.

When the furniture came in it had snow on top, and so did we. After the gas men had been to connect the gas stove Mum made tea. Everyone stood steaming in the kitchen.

I took Charlie up the stairs and sat him by the back window.

'Look, Charlie!' We'd never had a garden before.

It was knobbly white, with snow-striped fences. A gate at the bottom. Beyond another back garden, another house, in another road.

'Who lives there, I wonder?'

Somebody came out. Girl? Boy? Done up into a parcel, with a scarf for string, I couldn't tell.

The parcel ran towards our house. Popped up behind our gate. Climbed right over into our garden and . . . began making snowballs!

A man in a red scarf came up the alley between the houses. He turned towards our garden gate and . . .

SPLIT! Splat! Splot!

Snowballs burst on his chest. His head. They burst all over him. Then the parcel ran up our garden. Round and round in the snow, kicking and rolling. Laughing and whooping.

The man leaned on the gate and pointed. He pointed at me! The parcel looked up and saw me too. Girl? Boy? I still couldn't tell.

A moment later it was gone. Over the gate and up the other garden. Into the house, and the man in the red scarf too.

I went to find my bed.

It was all in bits and pieces, propped against the wall of a little room in the front. I'd never had a room of my own before.

Round the tops of the walls was a wallpaper shoe. It went on and on, even round the corners. And everywhere there were children. Sitting on the roof. Swinging from shoelaces. Climbing out of windows. Up and down drainpipes.

'There was an old woman . . . .' And there she was, sitting outside the door, over the heel.

Dad's head came round my bedroom door.

'Well, what do you think?'

I nodded. 'I like it.'

'When you can't get off to sleep you can count children instead of sheep.'

'I can only count to twenty-nine.'

'Things change,' Dad said.

The snow melted in the night.

Next day there was nothing left in the garden but gluggy blobs on wet brown earth.

A boy came walking early up the path. Was this the parcel?

Mum opened the kitchen door.

'Come to say sorry.' His pink face shone in the sun.

'Sorry for what?' Mum asked, but he couldn't say. Just shook his head and looked at his feet.

The man in the red scarf came next.

'Pat's said his piece?'

Mum smiled at Pat.

'He didn't know anybody had moved in, you see. And I was just coming off duty.' The man held out his hand. 'Cross. That's me.' Mum shook his hand. 'Haven't I seen you somewhere before?'

Then Dad came with a white clown's face. He pointed with his shaving brush.

'I know. You drove our bus.'

After Mr Cross had gone I put on my coat and went out in the garden with Pat.

'You haven't come far,' he said.

'I have.'

'Not on a Number 55 bus.'

'Before the bus there was a train. We've moved out of town.'

Pat sniffed and kicked at a lump of earth. 'You'll need to watch out round here.'

'What for?'

'You'll find out.'

We went down his alley, then on down his road.

Pat's was a proper finished road with all the houses lived in. After the last one he pointed to the empty stretch.

'See that? That's the swamps.'

All I could see was earth and grass and shining wet.

'You don't go there because you'd drown.'

'I'd swim.'

'You wouldn't. The swamps are full of weed and mud. They'd suck you down. You'd need feet . . . ten metres long at least.' He put one foot alongside mine. 'See what funny little feet you got?'

'I've got a shoe as long as the sides of a room.'

'You never.'

'I have, I have!'

'Wash out your mouth with soap and water!'

'It's *true*.'

'Show me then.'

We marched across the sticky earth to where the road began down Cuckoo Lane. And when we reached my house we marched upstairs.

Pat saw the shoe all round my room.

'That's a cheat!'

'No it isn't.'

He picked up Charlie, and dropped him on his head.

'Old town rabbit. My friend Mick has *real* rabbits.'

'I don't care.'

'I'm going home now,' Pat said. 'Now I've shown you what to watch out for.'

Mum stopped moving the furniture around.

'Well?' she asked. 'Have you made a friend?'

I wasn't sure.

'What do friends do?'

'Well . . . . Friends are friendly. Good to be with.'

'Do they show you what to watch out for?'

'Well . . . .'

'And argue all the time?'

Mum shook her head sadly. She'd just found all our mud.

I went upstairs to Charlie, and the shoe children. One of *them* would have to be my friend. I chose a girl with red ringlets, and her feet dangling out of a window. And called her Gloria.

2

. . . and Stole the Builder's Sand

One morning I woke and everything was shining.

The sun. The faces of the shoe children. They looked as though they'd all had a good scrub, and eaten up their Sunday breakfasts. Their cats prowled on the roof. The dogs sat on the doorstep. And the old woman knew exactly what to do. Make all those beds, and start on the washing-up.

'*You're* lucky,' I told Gloria. 'Sitting there, dangling your feet out of the window. What would happen if I did a thing like that?'

But Gloria was stuck on my wall for ever. I could go anywhere in the whole wide world. Down the stairs, out of my front door . . . .

No I couldn't. Not now. Skipper had come out of the front door opposite.

Skipper was never like the shoe children's dogs. He barked and jumped and snapped and nipped. And he belonged to Captain Cobley, who'd gone away to sea leaving Skipper behind to look after Mrs Cobley for him.

Down Cuckoo Lane the builder's men had been busy.

There was another new house next door. Then the alley. A half-built house the other side. And waiting for the builder's men on Monday morning an orange cement mixer. Ladders. Piles of bricks and tiles. Best of all, a mountain of sand.

The more I thought of the sand mountain the more I couldn't stop. Sand meant pies and castles. Think what the shoe children would have done with all that sand!

I went the back way.

Out of our garden gate, creeping quietly up the alley so Skipper wouldn't hear. The half-built house had no gate, no fence, no garden path. I just walked straight in.

My sand shoe house stretched from one wall to another. There were windows made of bits of wood. A chimney from a piece of gutter. The door above the heel was a tile. If only Gloria could have seen it.

When I went home Dad was in the kitchen making tea.

'Where've you been?'

'Nowhere special.' I hid my yellow hands behind my back.

After breakfast Dad went down to the bottom of the garden to dig a hole for a rubbish pit. When he wasn't looking I crept back up the alley.

'OH!'

The sand shoe had gone. Every bit of it. Vanished, as though it had never been!

Trip, trap. Trip, trap. I knew that sound. *Skipper was coming*!

It was too late to run. Perhaps, if I didn't move or breathe, he'd miss me . . . .

'Oy!'

Skipper hadn't turned into a talking dog. The voice had come from the window frame.

'Come out of there!'

I glared at Pat. 'Was it you knocked down my house?'

He nodded.

Scooping up a handful of sand I threw it.

The sand hit the window frame. When Pat

came up again his face was covered in freckles.

'Stop that!' Pat said angrily. 'Didn't I say you'd need to watch out? Mr Wood, the builder, comes Sunday mornings to see how his houses are getting along.'

But Pat had forgotten to watch out for Skipper, who went and nipped him on the leg.

In the afternoon Mum moved the furniture around. Again. Dad had to help. I was sent out of the way into the garden.

'Oy!'

I turned my back on Pat.

'Got something to show you.'

'What?'

'Come and see. *Come on*! I can't lift it up. It's too heavy.'

He was holding on to an empty wheelbarrow.

'We fill it, see?'

I shook my head.

'With sand, of course. Then we put it in your pit.'

'It's not my pit, it's Dad's.'

'Same thing. Listen. I'd make it in my garden, only it's full up already with little paths

18

and crazy paving.'

'But Dad's made the pit for rubbish.'

'What rubbish?' Pat looked round the empty garden. 'He'd be more pleased with a sand-pit. It's not everybody has the chance. I wish *I* had the chance. Your mum, she'll be pleased too. Keep you out of trouble. Like going and messing up Mr Wood's new house. You told her, have you?'

'No.'

'Just as well.'

He climbed the gate and helped himself to

Dad's shovel.

'Come on then.'

It was hard work loading the wheelbarrow. Skipper came and watched, but kept his distance.

'Here, you have a go.' Pat gave me the shovel.

I'd just got it full of sand and was trying to lift it when . . . .

'Caught you nicely, haven't I?'

'It's Mr Wood!' Pat said. 'Come in the afternoon instead of the morning!'

Mr Wood sent us to fetch our fathers.

Dad and Mr Cross came up the alley.

'So here you are,' boomed Mr Wood, for all the world to hear. 'The fine people who buy my houses. And send their children out to steal.'

Mr Cross reached for Pat.

'It was only to give her something to play with,' Pat protested. 'The poor little thing.'

'Who's a poor little thing?' Dad said.

Then Mum arrived, and turned her best smile on Mr Wood. While Mr Cross made Pat unload the wheelbarrow Mr Wood came into our house for a cup of tea.

Mum sent me to bed early.

I didn't really mind. The shoe children were going to bed too. They cleaned their teeth, and flicked toothpaste at each other. There were so many children they used up a whole tube every day. The old woman brushed their hair, and did Gloria's up in rags. And then I counted them.

Dad came in to say goodnight.

'What comes after twenty-nine?'

'Thirty.'

'And what comes after that?'

'Thirty-one.'

'And what . . . .'

'And what comes next is going to school.'

'I know. Will I like it?'

'Of course you will,' Dad said. 'And don't let anyone ever call you a poor little thing again.'

3
... and Started School as a Spotted Dick

The day I started school was a day to remember, and forget as quickly as possible.

The Saturday before Mum took me on a Number 55 bus to the stores to buy material. In between cooking Sunday dinner she cut out my new school dress. I sat under the table sticking pins back in the pin cushion. Then I folded up the pieces of paper pattern.

Dad clumped into the kitchen. He'd been planting out the garden, and was tired and hungry.

'Dinner's late,' Mum told him.

Dad liked things to happen on time. Especially important things, like Sunday dinner.

'Tomorrow is an important day,' Mum said.

Dad couldn't think why.

I came out from under the table. 'Silly old Dad. It's *school*.'

'Silly old school,' Dad said. 'And anyway,

why should school tomorrow mean late Sunday dinner today?'

We told him, but he still hung about the kitchen. Sniffing. Sighing. Prodding the vegetables.

'I wish you'd go away.' Mum didn't like cooking, and Sunday dinner least of all.

Dad went into the dining room where the table was covered with bits of material. Yellow, with blue spots.

'You'll look like a spotted dick,' Dad said.

We cleared the table, put on the cloth, and set out the knives and forks and spoons. I wouldn't have minded spotted dick for dinner, but it was just the same old rice pudding.

Afterwards Mum fetched out the sewing machine. Sometimes, on a long seam, I was allowed to turn the handle.

When the dress was ready for trying on I climbed up on a chair. I had to keep turning, like a merry-go-round, while Mum pinned up the hem. Sometimes she stuck pins in my legs by mistake.

On Monday morning Dad said, 'Good luck, Spotty,' and went off down Cuckoo Lane to

23

catch his Number 55 bus to the station. He left at the same time every morning. Mrs Cobley set her clock by him.

Next Mum and I put on our coats. After I'd run upstairs to say a last goodbye to Charlie and Gloria we started out.

Up Cuckoo Lane we went, and right into Greenfields Road. Past houses, shops, and houses again. On up Green Hill. By now there were a lot of children all walking in the same direction.

Pat came out of one of the houses with another boy.

'Now don't forget,' Mum told me. 'Pat will bring you home at dinnertime.' It had been arranged with Mrs Cross. 'You're to wait for him at the school gate.'

But dinnertime was hours away. Children were coming towards me, because we'd nearly reached the school. It was *now* I wanted to know about.

Hobday School. There was the name on the notice. We walked past it, and on up the drive. The playground was enormous. And round at the back a field that stretched for ever.

There was such a bustle inside I didn't notice Mum leave. My teacher, Miss Maybe, showed me my peg and I hung up my coat.

Pat had said he'd come and sit behind me, but he didn't. He wasn't even in my class. I didn't know any of the other children either.

'Now sit up straight with your hands in your laps,' said Miss Maybe.

After she'd called our names we had to draw a picture. I drew Gloria with her ringlets, but Miss Maybe thought it was a bonfire.

At playtime I saw Pat, with the boy who lived on Green Hill.

'Mick!' I heard Pat call him. 'Come on, Mick!' But he never called to me.

Nobody else did either. I looked down at the spotted dick dress with my blue socks sticking out of the bottom, just to make certain I was really there.

At dinnertime I went to fetch my coat. It had gone. It wasn't on any of the pegs. Outside it had begun to rain, but I hurried to the gate so as not to keep Pat waiting.

After everybody else had gone I saw Miss Maybe looking out. I didn't want her thinking

I was a poor little thing who couldn't walk home alone, so off I went.

The hill was steep and made me puff. And the rain was coming down in buckets. The new dress had gone a funny colour. Pudding brown, with the spots turned black. Just like a real spotted dick!

I began to run, but then couldn't see where I was going. Once I went down a wrong road by mistake and had to come back to Green Hill again.

'Oy! You! Crackpot!'

Through the wet was a boy at a window. Pat's friend, Mick.

He called again, and a door opened. But coming towards me, nearly on top of me, under her second-best umbrella was . . . Mum!

'Trust you! I'd like to pick you up and wring you out!' She pulled me under the umbrella. '*Where is your coat?*'

'D-don't know.'

A new voice came from behind us.

'Come inside, *do*.'

Mum looked past me, shaking her head. 'It's very kind, but I have to get her home, and fed, and back to school again . . . .'

But all the same, a few moments later we were dripping all over Mick's kitchen floor.

'Pat Cross was supposed to bring her home.'

'And he forgot.' Mick's mother didn't sound surprised. 'That boy would forget an elephant standing on his foot!'

And suddenly Mum wasn't angry any more, but laughing with the rest of us.

Mick's mother wrapped me in a towel. She sent Mick for some of his clothes, and dropped my wet ones in the sink.

After being rubbed dry I was dressed in Mick's vest and pants and socks. His brown Saturday corduroy trousers and jumper. He was older than me. As old as Pat, and as tall and big. I wasn't a spotted dick any more but a galumphing chocolate pudding.

Mick's mother wanted to feed us, but Mum had left a stew on the gas.

I slopped along behind her in Mick's old gum boots. As we went out on to Green Hill Mr Cross drove up in his Number 55 bus.

The bus conductor thought I was a boy.

'What's happened to him?' he asked.

'Shrunk,' Mum said tartly.

When the bus stopped at the top of Cuckoo Lane Mr Cross leaned over for a better view.

'Don't look,' Mum ordered, turning her face towards Cuckoo Lane. 'We've had enough of those Crosses for one day.'

The stew had stuck to the saucepan and burnt, but I was so hungry I would have eaten anything. After changing my clothes it was time to hurry back to school again.

Miss Maybe said, 'Tut-tut,' when she heard what had happened.

In the afternoon I learnt a song and listened to a story about a magic pudding.

My coat was in the cloakroom again at hometime. Perhaps it was magic. But it was Miss Maybe who made certain I was inside it.

Mum was waiting. The sun was shining as we walked up the hill and stopped at Mick's house. After swopping my clothes back again we stayed to tea. Mick showed me his rabbits. One was called Bully Boy, and that's what he was. The other was Daisy, and she was lovely.

But the best thing that came of the day I started school was that Mum had made a friend. By the time we went home to Cuckoo Lane Mick's mother was my Auntie Maggie.

4
. . . and Gave the Builder's Wife Hysterics

Mum had moved the furniture round again.

I walked into a cupboard by mistake. Dad bumped into a table. And his dinner wasn't ready.

'Enough is enough,' Dad said.

'It's not enough for me,' said Mum, 'to be cooped up in a house all day.'

More and more often we went after school to Auntie Maggie's.

Auntie Maggie was a dressmaker. Her house was full of dressmaking things. Rolls of material. Reels of cotton. Pins. Patterns. Buttons. Her sewing machine had a room to itself. Also it had a treadle. A big metal plate, to work with your feet. Mick showed me how, but I couldn't do it.

'You're useless.'

'No I'm not.'

'Can't even work a sewing machine.'

'I can, I can. I work my mum's.'

'That tiddly little thing with a handle?'

'It's not tiddly.'

'Yes it is.'

He was a worse arguer than Pat.

When ladies came for fittings Mick was sent out of the room. I was allowed to stay and hold the pin cushion. Auntie Maggie never stuck pins in anybody.

One afternoon a girl came with her mother. The girl was older than me, older than Mick, and her name was Beryl. She walked into Auntie Maggie's house with her nose in the air. And there it stayed. Even when she climbed on a chair to have her hem pinned up.

'Turn around, Beryl,' her mother said. Beryl looked haughtily at the ceiling, and turned. 'Isn't she a picture?'

'Isn't she awful?' Mick said, after the girl and her mother had gone.

He climbed on a chair, made a haughty face, and turned around with his nose in the air.

'How did *you* know that was what she did?'

'I was watching through the keyhole.'

We went to see Bully Boy and Daisy.

While I was trying to feed Daisy a lettuce leaf

Mick said, 'You know who she is, don't you?'

'Yes,' I said. 'Daisy.'

'I mean the girl, you crackpot.' Mick took Bully Boy out of the cage, to give Daisy a chance at the lettuce.

'I know that too. Beryl.'

'Of course she's Beryl.' Mick jumped back as Bully Boy kicked him. 'She's also Mr Wood, the builder's daughter. Stay still, you pesky rabbit!'

But Bully Boy escaped, and we rushed off after him. Next door lived a large watchful cat, which kept a large watchful eye on Bully Boy.

Next time Beryl came she was to be a bridesmaid, and her elder sister the bride.

'To think of it.' Mrs Wood, the builder's wife, sank into a chair. 'My baby. Married!'

'You still have Beryl,' Auntie Maggie said.

'And what her father will do without her . . . .'

'He still has Beryl too.'

'Beryl isn't old enough to do his office work. And if there's one thing Mr Wood hates it's being cooped up in an office.'

'Cooped up?' Auntie Maggie looked

thoughtful.

Mrs Wood licked her thumb and turned the pages of the pattern book. Beryl looked out of the window.

A few days went by. Then Mum said, 'Go in to Auntie Maggie's after school. I'll be along to fetch you later.'

Beryl came for a fitting.

Mick put his nose in the air and walked into a doorpost. He made me giggle, and I couldn't stop. Auntie Maggie sent us both away.

We went to feed the rabbits.

Bully Boy was being his usual nasty self. Mick took him out of the cage, and of course he escaped. But instead of charging off into the garden he ran inside the house.

As Mick chased after him I looked through the keyhole at Beryl.

'She does look beautiful. In spite of her nose. Mrs Wood has tears in her eyes. And your mum is nearly crying too.'

'Let me see.' Mick pushed me aside. I leaned my back against the door to let him look, and . . . .

Mrs Wood screamed as we flew inside, but

not because of us.

'Ee! Eee! *Take it away! Eeee!*'

The builder's wife clutched her skirt and wrapped it tight around her legs. Bully Boy ran over the top of her feet, then disappeared inside a roll of material.

'*EEEEEEEEEEEE . . .*' screamed Mrs Wood.

As for Beryl . . . . Her nose came down and her mouth opened wide. But *she* didn't scream. Oh no! She laughed and laughed and laughed and laughed. As though she hadn't laughed for a very long time, and might never find anything to laugh at ever again. And the more Beryl laughed the louder her mother screamed.

'How can we stop them?' Auntie Maggie looked at Mick. He looked at me. And I looked at . . . the pin cushion.

'Oh no. I couldn't!' said Auntie Maggie.

'You could.' Mick nodded. 'It's either that, or a bucket of water.'

'And ruin that lovely material?'

Auntie Maggie took out two pins, and jabbed.

When the noise cut off our heads still rang.

The whole house rang. Mick captured Bully Boy and put him back in his cage. Auntie Maggie made Mrs Wood a strong cup of tea.

After that Beryl stopped being snooty. She never exactly spoke to Mick or me, but she always looked in our direction.

The very next week Mum started work in Mr Wood's office, so neither of them need be cooped up any more.

Dad's dinner wasn't *always* on time. But the furniture was never moved around again.

5
... and Was Farmed Out

Spring had come and everyone was busy. Mum was working for Mr Wood, the builder. Down Cuckoo Lane the new houses reached nearly to the swamps.

Up on Green Hill Auntie Maggie was making spring dresses. Her big treadle sewing machine never stopped. School days I went to her for my dinners. And afternoons until Mum came to fetch me.

Mum was worried about Auntie Maggie.

'She's looking as pale as silk,' she told Dad.

'Cooking other children's dinners doesn't help,' he said.

Mrs Thresher, in the house next door, popped up the other side of the garden fence.

'I can give the poor little dear her dinners.'

Dad frowned. He didn't like people who listened behind fences. And he hated me being called a poor little dear. But Mum smiled politely at Mrs Thresher.

The next school dinnertime I went next door.

Mr Thresher was there as well. A rumbly man with pouty lips, eating his dinner and reading his newspaper. Banging the table with his fist, making the salt and pepper jump.

I was glad when he went. Slamming the door behind him.

'He can't abide children,' Mrs Thresher told me. And then she started asking questions.

It was the same the next day, and the next. Rumble. Pout. Bang. Wallop. Then questions, questions, questions . . . .

'What does your daddy like best to eat?'

Was Mrs Thresher thinking of feeding him as well?

'Rice pudding,' I told her.

'And does your mummy cook it for him?'

'Every Sunday,' I said politely. Mum had told me always to be polite.

'*Every* Sunday?'

'Yes.'

'And what does your mummy like best to eat?'

'I don't know. Yes, I do. Chocolate éclairs.'

Another day she'd seen Dad's telescope
sticking out of an upstairs window.

'What was your daddy doing?'

'Looking at the sky.' Dad liked to look at
stars and planets, to give him a change from
people.

'And does he often?' Mrs Thresher asked.

'Often what?' It wasn't easy *always* being
polite.

'Look through his telescope.'

'Yes, he does. Especially now you're here.'

Down Cuckoo Lane people whispered as we

passed by.

'What's the matter with them all?' Mum couldn't understand it.

Dad went and looked through his telescope at the Milky Way.

Then Pat came up to me in the playground.

'Is your dad really a spy?'

'No. He's an optician.'

'He's got a telescope though, hasn't he?'

'Yes.'

'And he watches people through it.'

'Of course he doesn't. He looks at the sky. Last night he looked at the Milky Way.'

'I suppose that's what comes of having to eat rice pudding every Sunday. While your mum goes out to work so she can live off chocolate éclairs.'

'Who told you that?'

'Mrs Thresher told my mum. And Mrs Thresher knows everything.'

That evening I told Mum I didn't want to go next door for my dinners any more.

'Why not?'

'They're horrible.'

'Trust you,' Mum said.

Next I went to the family the other side of the alley.

It was a big family of big people. They ate so much I couldn't believe it. Mountain ranges of greens and potatoes. Meaty swamps. Puddings like cities. Rivers of custard.

I was sick three days in a row.

'Trust you,' Mum said.

After that came Mrs Cobley. And Mrs Cobley's dinners were exactly right. She never asked me questions either. Just told me stories about Captain Cobley.

There were pictures of ships in every room. Ships in port. Ships in storms. Ships on calm flat seas, and out on the wide dark ocean. There was even a ship in a bottle.

But . . . . There was Skipper.

When Mrs Cobley wasn't looking he'd nip my legs. Snap at my fingers. Barge me aside with his fat black body. Roll his wicked brown eyes, and growl. Captain Cobley had told Skipper to take good care of Mrs Cobley while he was away at sea. And he was going to.

One day I dropped a lump of potato. It landed on Mrs Cobley's shoe. I crawled under the table, put out my hand and . . . .

'OW!'

'Trust you,' Mum said when she saw my finger, done up in a bandage like a fat white sausage.

But Dad frowned deeply.

'I want you to tell me . . . .'

Mum gave a very long sigh.

' . . . have you had enough?'

'Enough?'

'Of being farmed out.'

'What's that?' I asked.

'Going here, there and everywhere for your dinners.'

'No, I like it.'

Mum jumped up and hugged me.

For a while I went to Mrs Cross. But there was Pat to look out for. And his elder brothers and sisters, who nicked the best bits off each other's plates.

'You bolt your food too fast,' Dad grumbled.

But Mum said it didn't matter. Auntie Maggie's spring rush was over, and she wanted me to go back there for my dinners. So that was the end of being farmed out.

6
. . . and Became an Assistant

The family the other side of the alley had a bike. In turn they whizzed down Cuckoo Lane, then struggled up to their house again.

I watched, and wished. Their bike was too big for me. But Mum said one of my own would have to wait.

'What for?'

'An occasion.'

'What's an occasion?'

'Your birthday. Christmas.'

'But they're ages away.' I looked at the clock, wishing I could make it hurry up. 'Oh, Mum. If only . . . .'

'If only you'd stop bothering me. Your father and I have quite enough to bother us already.'

But things that bother grown-ups are rarely worth listening to. So I didn't. Until . . . .

' . . . her little girl is ill,' Dad said.

'Whose little girl?' I asked.

'Don't interrupt,' Mum snapped.

'I really need my assistant,' Dad said. 'Saturday is my busy day.'

'It's mine as well.' Mum sighed. 'I have to call in at the office. Fetch all the shopping. And there's the weekly wash, and . . . .' Mum stared at me. 'What does your assistant *do*?'

'Check people in and out. Answer the telephone. See to the post.'

'Money for jam. A child could do it.'

'I'm a child,' I said.

Next morning Dad and I set off down Cuckoo Lane. Skipper barked. Mrs Cobley waved, and went to check her clock.

Mr Cross drove up in his Number 55 bus. Dad and I went on top in front. As we passed Hobday School I sat up straight with my hands in my lap. What would Miss Maybe say if she knew I was off to Dad's shop to become an assistant?

At Greenfields Station we got off the bus and caught the tube.

When we came out into the world again we walked to Dad's optician's shop.

He unlocked the door and the bell went

ping! I went inside and turned the notice from
CLOSED to OPEN.

The floor smelt of polish. The glass counter
shone. Spectacles gleamed in the morning sun.

Ping!

There stood the milkman with a bottle of
milk.

The workroom had a musty smell. With its
grinding machine, and packets of lenses. Spec-
tacle cases and little boxes. A kettle on a gas
ring, and an old brown teapot.

Ping!

This time it was the postman.

'Oh ho!' he said. 'Got ourselves a new assistant?'

'Yes,' I said. 'It's me.'

I gave Dad the letters and boxes he'd
brought, and went into the testing room. This
was the best place of all.

Black as night. A chair like a throne, which
whizzed up and down. Alphabet letters on the
wall behind, large at the top and small below.
Opposite a great big mirror. I pressed a switch
and the light shone green.

'Stop playing about,' Dad came and told

44

me. 'You're here to work.'

'What shall I do?'

'Listen, and I'll tell you . . . .'

The shop bell went *ping*! The telephone rang. Customers came, and customers went.

'Hold the line,' I had to say into the telephone.

'Sit down, please,' to the people who came to have their eyes tested.

Once I got muddled and said, 'Sit down, please,' into the telephone.

'I am sitting down,' said the voice. 'Who is that?'

'The . . . astician's opsistant.'

'And I'm the Queen of the Fairies! Goodbye!'

Ping!

A boy called Alec came in with his mother. He was thin and pale, and his clothes were darned. He never smiled.

When he went in the testing room I peeped inside.

Alec's thin legs were hanging in space. Dad spun the chair and whirled him round. Alec held on tight, but he never smiled. And he couldn't read many of the letters on the wall either.

'You should have brought him sooner,' Dad told Alec's mother. 'He needs spectacles badly.'

She took out her purse, but Dad shook his head.

'There's no charge,' he said quietly.

Then Alec smiled. And Dad told him he'd look very smart in his new spectacles, and they'd be ready in two weeks' time.

When it was one o'clock I turned the notice from OPEN to CLOSED. Dad lit the gas ring under the kettle, and brought out the sandwiches from home.

Scritch, scratch. Scritch, scratch.

'What is it, Dad?'

He went and unbolted the workroom door.

A dog came in.

'Oh, Dad. I don't like dogs.'

'You'll like this one. It's Bob, from the eel and pie shop.'

Bob was brown, with eyes like treacle. He raised a shaggy paw.

'Don't disappoint him,' Dad said. 'He wants

46

to shake hands.'

So I had to.

Then Dad poured some tea into a saucer and Bob drank it down in noisy splashes. Afterwards he ate my crusts. Dad had a doze and Bob leaned against him, closing his eyes.

When I was sure they were both asleep I crept away. In the testing room I turned on the green light and made froggy faces in the mirror. Then I sat on the throne, and whizzed it up. Round and round. Higher and higher. Until it would turn no more. Then....

Everything went black. And a large furry

body landed on top of me!

I couldn't move the chair with Bob in it too. We'd just have to stay there until Dad came to find us.

It was very hot squashed next to Bob. Sometimes he licked my face, and it was funny and tickly. Because it was so dark my eyes thought it was bedtime. I began to think of Gloria and the shoe children . . . .

'*What on earth . . . ?*'

'Hello, Dad.'

I stepped out of the chair, but . . . the floor wasn't there!

Dad was angry.

'You might have broken your silly neck!'

Bob began to lick my face. 'And as for you!' Dad told him. When Bob had come in and jumped up to the chair his back leg must have pulled out the light plug.

The chair was wound down. Bob was sent home. The notice turned from CLOSED to OPEN. And off we went again.

Time moved so slowly that day. But at last I stuck the stamps on Dad's letters and boxes. Turned the notice from OPEN to CLOSED.

How tired I was, and glad to finish being an assistant.

While Dad was locking up I went and looked in the eel and pie shop.

There was a man in a dirty striped apron chopping up eels. Pies stacked up like Dad's little boxes. Bob came out of the eel and pie shop. He held up his paw and we said goodbye.

'I wish . . . ' I said as we walked to the station. 'I wish that Bob was mine.'

'How can he be yours when he belongs to the eel and pie man?'

'Is the eel and pie man kind to Bob?'

'Very kind,' Dad said.

'Then why isn't he kind to eels?'

'Because people like to eat them.'

'I don't,' I said. 'And I won't ever.'

Dad gave me the letters and boxes to put in the postbox. We caught the tube to Greenfields Station, and the Number 55 bus, and came home.

Not long after Dad brought me home a box. It wasn't one of his little ones either.

'Your wages,' he said. 'For being my assistant.'

49

The box was heavy.

'Is it money?'

'If it was,' Mum said, 'we'd be living in a castle. Not here, down Cuckoo Lane.'

'Then what is it?'

'There's only one way to find out.'

I opened up the box. Inside was . . . a bike.

7
. . . and Found a Best Friend

I rode and rode and rode my bike. Down Cuckoo Lane, and up again. There was Skipper to dodge. And Pat. But Pat was always off somewhere with his best friend, Mick. I wished I could find a best friend.

One hometime Auntie Maggie was a long time coming to open her front door.

'Oh, it's you,' she said in a funny voice, and looked past me. 'Where's Mick?'

'I don't know.'

'And I don't know how I'm going to tell him.'

'Tell him what?'

But Auntie Maggie couldn't say. She just closed the door behind me and led the way into the garden. There was Daisy, nibbling daintily on a lettuce leaf. But where was Bully Boy?

'Gone.' Auntie Maggie gave a moan and put her head in her hands.

I went at once and looked all round the garden. What was Auntie Maggie so worked up about? Mick would be cross, but if I could find Bully Boy before he came home . . . .

'You may look,' said Auntie Maggie. 'But you'll never find him.'

'Why not?'

'That horrible cat next door has . . . eaten him.'

The watchful cat? 'He *can't* have!'

But it was true.

I cried. Auntie Maggie cried. Then we heard Mick coming.

Auntie Maggie wiped her eyes and mine. 'We have to be brave. For Mick's sake.'

We went to the front door together.

Mick came in with a great big appetite. 'Where's my tea? I want it *now*.' And never a thought for anything else.

I helped Auntie Maggie get the tea quickly.

Mick took the bread with the most butter, and ate it all up. Then helped himself to the biggest slice of cake, and ate all that up too.

'Pat's gone to the dentist's,' he announced. '*He* won't get any tea.'

Then he stared at my legs dangling from my chair.

'Do you know something? Your legs are different sizes.'

He fetched Auntie Maggie's tape measure, and it was true. One of my legs was a whole inch fatter than the other.

'Do you know something else?' Mick said. 'You're peculiar.'

I nodded.

He frowned. 'What's the matter with you? Why don't you say, "I'm not, I'm not"?' Mick turned on his mother. '*And why don't you tell me off?*'

Auntie Maggie turned away.

'There's something funny going on.' Mick went into the garden. He came back running. 'Where's Bully Boy? I know. *She's* let him out, hasn't she? And now she can't find him. And if Bully Boy gets into next door's garden . . . .'

'He did get into next door's garden,' Auntie Maggie said bravely. 'After he'd escaped from his cage. He scratched his way out. You know Bully Boy. At least . . . you did know Bully Boy.'

53

When Mick discovered what had happened he tore about like a wild thing.

One moment he was out in the garden. Next he was up the stairs. We heard the sewing machine going. And all the time he was shouting and shouting.

Then he took Daisy out of her cage. He went and sat with her in the far corner of the garden. And sobbed, and sobbed, and sobbed.

'Leave him alone,' said Mum when she came to collect me. 'Let him get over it in his own way.'

In the playground next day Mick told everybody. How the cat next door was twice as fat, and still hadn't moved from the place where he'd caught and eaten Bully Boy. He even told Miss Maybe.

'What's up with *her*?' Dad asked when he came home from the shop.

Mum glanced at me. 'I expect it's that rabbit.'

'Is it that rabbit?'

'Yes,' I said. 'And one of my legs is fatter than the other.'

Mum looked at them closely.

'It's true. It must be the way she rides that bike.'

'Well, ride it properly,' Dad said. 'And forget about the rabbit.'

I drew a picture of Bully Boy, so I never would forget him. Then I fetched out my bike.

The reason I didn't ride it properly was the hill. Going down was lovely. But coming up I kept stopping, and falling off. So I pushed hard on the ground with one leg . . . .

I tried so hard not to stop that I didn't see what was coming.

WALLOP!

A table fell on top of me. There were feet all round, and a big van by the kerb. I'd ridden my bike into people moving in.

One of the removal men picked up the bike and propped it against the wall.

'Now then, girlie. You keep out of the way.'

There was another girl sitting on the wall. A sideboard was coming out of the van, so I went and sat next to her. We looked at each other, then looked away, and watched the furniture going in.

Next day when I rode down the hill the girl was there again.

I sat on the wall and we looked at each other, and looked away. Then the girl said, 'I haven't got a bike.'

'You can have a ride on mine.'

So she did. Later on she came to tea. She saw Charlie, the drawing of Bully Boy and the children in the shoe. And she liked them all.

Afterwards we went into the garden.

Pat hung over the gate at the bottom and whistled.

'Who's he?' the new girl asked.

'Pat Cross.'

'Why is he whistling like that?'

'Because he's got a gap in his teeth.'

She picked a privet leaf and blew it. Pat came in and blew leaves too. He told her to watch out for the swamps. Skipper. And Miss Maybe.

My new friend shook her head and smiled. 'Miss Maybe is a friend of Mum and Dad's.'

'But she's a teacher,' said Pat.

'So is my dad. He's going to teach at Hobday School. So it's you who'd better watch out.'

Miss Maybe let my new friend sit next to me in class. We walked to school together every morning.

In her house there was a grandmother who wore a black velvet band round her neck, and knitted with one needle tucked under her arm. And there was a ginger cat called Fred.

My legs were never quite the same size again, but I couldn't be bothered any more. Not now I'd found a best friend.

8
. . . and Came by Tadpoles

My best friend's father was making a pond.

He put in rushes, waterlilies, and goldfish. The next day the goldfish had gone.

Fred, my best friend's cat, lay on the grass. He warmed his furry orange tum in the warm spring sunshine. He purred . . . and sometimes he burped.

More goldfish were put in the pond. And went.

Next a net was placed over the water. But what was the good of a pond you couldn't peer into? Dip in your fingers and flick water about? So the net went too. And so did the next lot of goldfish.

'Yer pays yer money, and yer takes yer choice,' said my best friend's father. Which sounded very strange, since he was a teacher.

My best friend put her arms round Fred, who scratched all down the side of her face. But what were a few pretty fish compared with a furry, purry, scratchy cat?

Then my best friend's grandmother, knitting in a deckchair, said, 'Tadpoles.'

'Aha!' My best friend's father pointed at Fred. 'Some jumping frogs might teach you a lesson, my lad.'

'Frogs aren't tadpoles,' my best friend said.

'To start with they are. They grow into frogs later. Now where can we come by some tadpoles?'

The next day, Sunday, I woke up early.

Gloria sat on the roof in the sunshine, her red ringlets shining. Outside in the road somebody was whistling.

I ran to the window.

Where was Pat going so early? And why was he carrying a jam jar on a string?

Later on, after breakfast, I went down Cuckoo Lane to call for my best friend.

Behind the gardens on that side of the road was rough wild land called the jungle. On the edge of the jungle, by a slimy ditch, tall trees grew. From the tree behind my best friend's house hung a rope with a knot on the end.

59

We took turns to sit on the knot, and swing. And sooner or later one of us would say, 'Now let's play Ghost Rides.'

It was our own special game. The swinger closed her eyes, while the other one pushed and did ghostly things. Flapped floppy leaves in her face. Brushed her arms and legs with grasses. Made terrible blood-curdling wails. Or horrible ghostly groans. And the swinger never opened her eyes, whatever.

That Sunday the scary bit never got going. I swung and swung and swung and swung . . . .

'Go on, push!'

Nothing happened.

'*Do something.* If you don't I'll open my eyes.'

Still nothing.

I was just about to open them when . . . .

WHOOMPH! Off I went again!

'Not so hard,' I shouted, but . . . .

WHOOMPH!

Whoomph!!

Whoomph!!!

I was swinging higher than ever before. Had my best friend gone bananas?

Then on my next swing backwards I heard a

whistle. Opening my eyes I saw two jam jars down at the base of the tree.

'Ow!' yelled a solid lump of boy as I dropped off on top of him.

'Where's my best friend?' I asked, after we'd sorted ourselves out.

'Captured.' Pat ran down into the slimy ditch, then up the other side. 'And you're dead,' he said when I followed him.

'I'm not.'

'You are. You didn't watch out, and just fell into a big swollen river.'

'I didn't, I didn't.'

'You did, you did. You've been swept away. You're not here at all.'

'You fell in too!'

'I'm a champion swimmer, so I'm all right.'

My best friend was in her garden tied to the clothes pole. There was a pillowcase over her head, and Mick was doing a war dance.

Fred came prowling down the path.

'There's a big wild beast.' Mick prodded the pillowcase. 'Coming to finish you off.'

An angry buzz came out of the pillowcase.

I ran and untied my best friend. Under the

pillowcase she had a white thing tied round her mouth. Her grandmother's summer vest!

Mick and Pat vanished into the jungle. But after we'd pegged the pillowcase and vest back on the line we found they'd forgotten the jam jars.

Inside was water, and little dark brown darting things. We took them to my best friend's father.

'Just the job. Tadpoles.'

'How can they be tadpoles?' my best friend asked. 'They're not a bit like frogs.'

'Not yet. But just you watch.'

He emptied the jam jars into the pond. Fred came to watch, but the tadpoles were too quick for him.

After we'd put the empty jam jars back under the tree we hurried back to the pond. We watched all day. The tadpoles stayed the same, but by the end of the day the jam jars had gone.

On Monday Pat and Mick caught us in the playground.

'Murderers!' said Mick.

'Tadpole killers!' said Pat.

'We're not. We're not.'

'Where are they then?' Mick pulled my arms behind my back. 'Did you feed them to that orange beast?'

'We didn't. We didn't.'

'If you really want to know,' my best friend said in a haughty voice. 'The tadpoles are living in our pond. Turning into frogs.'

Next Sunday Pat and Mick came to see for themselves. The tadpoles had grown bigger. Some even had little legs. Pat and Mick were so pleased they asked us to go with them over the swamps to get some more.

We wanted to go, but we weren't allowed.

Perhaps it was just as well. Mick sank, and lost one of his gum boots. Pat dropped his jam jar coming home, and all his tadpoles went down the drain.

Mick put his in my best friend's pond with the others. They all grew into lovely little hopping frogs. And for all I know their ancestors are there to this very day.

9
... *and Had to be a Rotten Rose*

Cuckoo Lane is a strange name for a road in a built-up area. But it wasn't all built-up then. There really were cuckoos. Not perched on the rooftops, like sparrows or starlings. But flapping about in the trees of the jungle.

Whenever they began their cuckoo-ing I put my head in the air to listen. And when I did it going fast on my bike down Cuckoo Lane . . . .

CRASH!

'Eurgh!' said my best friend when she saw me.

Her mother wiped away the blood, and put a plaster on.

Next day I fell over on my way to school. That wasn't the cuckoos' fault but my new summer sandals', which had soles like dinner plates. Blood dripped into my socks, and down one arm.

'Eurgh!' My best friend looked away.

Mick came running out of his house.

'EURGH! You'll bleed to death!' He looked in my face to see how pale I was getting. Then Auntie Maggie came out and took me into her house.

My best friend came too. In spite of not wanting to look she wouldn't leave me. We waited while Auntie Maggie cleaned me up. And put more plasters on. Now I had four. One on my thin leg. Two on my fat leg. And another on my elbow.

By the time we went on down to Hobday School there wasn't another child in sight.

'We must hurry up,' my best friend said. But it wasn't easy with four plasters, and dinner plates for feet.

As we crossed the playground we met Miss Baloni.

The nearest we usually came to Miss Baloni was sitting on the hall floor in morning assembly. Miss Baloni was our headmistress. She was tall, like a bent beanpole. Her hair was black, scraped back in a bun. And she wore black-rimmed spectacles, with black eyes inside.

Even Mick and Pat were afraid of

66

Miss Baloni.

Very Naughty Children were seen waiting outside her room. And after they'd been inside they were never quite the same again.

My best friend and I found we were holding hands.

'Late!' snapped Miss Baloni. 'Why your mothers can't send you off in good time I really don't know. Or have you been loitering?'

'No, Miss Baloni.'

I wasn't certain what 'loitering' meant. And nor probably was my best friend.

Then Miss Baloni saw the plasters. You'd have thought I'd fallen over on purpose, and my best friend wasn't let off either.

'Did you have to stay and watch?'

'Yes, Miss Baloni. I mean, no, Miss Baloni.'

The headmistress leaned lower, and pointed to our classroom.

'HURRY!'

Miss Maybe tutted as we tottered in. 'What a pity. Now you've spoilt your attendance records. But at least you're in time for assembly.'

It was a special assembly that day. Miss

Baloni had something important to tell us.

'Hobday School is putting on a summer pageant,' she said.

'A padgint?' Pat did one of his funny whistles, and was sent to stand out at the side with a red face.

'The whole school will take part.' Miss Baloni bent and peered. 'Including you, Pat Cross. And I shall invite the Mayor to come and watch.'

When we got back to our classroom Miss Maybe told us that our class would be flowers and toadstools.

'What sort of flower are you going to be?' Mum asked that afternoon.

'A rotten rose. A rotten *pink* rose.'

Mum's face sank. 'You don't have a pink dress.'

'That's all right. I can be a toadstool instead. In my vest and knickers, with a tray on my head.'

'You'll be a pink rose,' Mum said firmly.

'And I will make the dress,' said Auntie Maggie. 'I have some rose pink taffeta that will be just right.'

I really hated that dress. It had sleeves like puff-balls, and the skirt stuck out all round. Some rose!

'Perhaps she'll look more rose-like when she loses her plasters,' Dad said.

But as fast as I lost them I kept on getting more.

'Trust you,' Mum told me.

'It's not my fault. It's these rotten sandals.'

'Rotten. *Rotten?* Will you stop using that word! And why can't you get on with your sandals like everybody else?'

'It's the rotten sandals that can't get on with *me.*'

'Well, I can't afford new ones. I'm saving up for our holiday.'

'Perhaps we could afford matching rose pink plaster,' Dad said.

Even my best friend's father had heard about me.

'You'll have to watch where you put your plates of meat,' he said.

But as I pushed my bike up the hill Skipper came barking . . . .

CRASH!

'That's our very last plaster!' Mum took my bike and locked it away.

Next day I watched my plates of meat all the way to school. But at breaktime . . . .

WALLOP!

There was blood all over. It was the worst fall yet. But worse was yet to come. I was sent to Miss Baloni's room. ALONE!

I knocked on the door. A voice said, 'Come.'

Miss Baloni looked me up and down. 'Not a pretty sight,' she said, and moved towards the alcove.

Pat had told me about the alcove where the sick and wounded went. There was a bed inside. A sink, and a box with a big red cross on it.

'And she tells you you're a warrior. Then she opens the box and takes out a bottle of stuff that's bright yellow. She tells you to be brave, but the yellow stuff stings worse than a thousand bees.'

'Did it make you cry?'

'Not me.' But there'd been inky marks, like blots, on Pat's pink face.

Miss Baloni beckoned, and I went and sat on

the bed.

'You're a real little warrior, aren't you?'

'Yes, Miss Baloni.'

She opened the box with the big red cross. Took out some cotton wool and wiped away the blood. She peered through her spectacles at my cuts and grazes. Perhaps they weren't so bad. Perhaps . . . .

'You're going to be a brave girl, aren't you?'

'Yes, Miss Baloni.'

She opened a bottle and . . . the yellow stuff was every bit as bad as Pat had said.

'I didn't, I didn't,' I told myself, as I went back down the corridor.

But just before reaching Miss Maybe's classroom I collided with a fly. By the time I'd rubbed it out of my eye nobody would believe I hadn't cried.

The day of the pageant Mum took off my plasters. Seven.

Ouch. Ouch! *Ouch!* OUCH. OUCH! *OUCH! OUCH!!*

'Trust you,' she said. 'Now listen. These are the latest invention.' She held out a packet. 'And very expensive. *Invisible* plasters. But they're not so strong as the old ones, so whatever you do, don't touch them.'

The Mayor came to the pageant wearing his chain. Mums and dads. Grandmothers and grandfathers. Friends and relations. Everybody was there. Mum asked Mrs Cobley. And my town aunts came in their best summer dresses.

'WELCOME TO YOU ALL,' said Miss Baloni.

She had ordered the sun to shine specially, so it did. It shone over the packed school field. On the flowers and toadstools. Elves and fairies. Pat and Mick were elves. On the lasses and lads. On Miss Maybe, a shepherdess. And my best friend's father, who was a swineherd.

The sun never let up for a moment. And one by one my plasters came unstuck, and dropped all over the field.

'A poor old ragged rose,' as Dad said afterwards.

'A rotten rose!' I dug my toes in the ground . . . and fell over.

Mum put the sandals away. I wore my plimsolls instead and when all my scabs had gone I got my bike back.

By that time the cuckoos had stopped cuckoo-ing. My best friend's father said they'd laid their eggs in other birds' nests. And now they were so ashamed of themselves they were keeping quiet.

... and Was Adopted by a Cat Called Venus

One Saturday a cat walked in.

It stayed all day, and I didn't go out once. Not even down Cuckoo Lane to my best friend's.

'I want to keep it,' I told Mum.

'But what about its owner? It's far too fat to be a stray.'

'Of course it's fat.' Mrs Thresher bobbed up like a jack-in-the-box. 'It's expecting.'

'Expecting what?' I asked.

'Kittens, of course.' Mrs Thresher shot my mother a triumphant look. 'And you'll be landed with them.'

The cat fixed her eyes on Mum and gave the most pitiful yowl.

We heard our front door open and close. Dad was home from the shop.

He came into the garden and stroked the cat, who rubbed her head against his legs.

74

'You're a nice little fellow.'

'He's not. He's a she,' Mum said. An important cough came from behind the fence. 'And she's expecting.'

We went indoors, and the cat came too. Where had she come from? Had she really been turned out because somebody didn't want the bother of her kittens?

Dad stroked the cat's head gently.

'She can stay with us, can't she, Dad?'

'Trust you,' Mum said. 'Haven't I enough to do without adopting a family of kittens?'

She wrote out two notices. One she pinned to a tree in Cuckoo Lane, and the other in Pat's road. The notices said: FOUND: BLACK FEMALE CAT. APPLY 54 CUCKOO LANE.

Days went by, but nobody did.

Dad called her Venus after his favourite planet. Mum lined a cardboard box with newspaper, and left it ready under the verandah.

One morning there were four little blind kittens in the box with Venus.

Each day my best friend and I watched

Venus feed them. We saw their eyes open. And their little bodies grow bigger and stronger. Sometimes Pat and Mick came and played with them too. We argued over the kittens' names. Except for the smallest, and he was Pluto.

One afternoon Mick came with a bulge in his pocket. Daisy.

'You stupid twit!' Pat told him. 'Remember what happened to Bully Boy?'

'Daisy is different. Daisy is lazy. Daisy wouldn't say boo to a goose.'

'What's she doing now then?'

A very strange noise was coming out of Mick's pocket.

Snuffle. Buzz! *Snuffle! BUZZ!*

'*There's a bee in with Daisy!*'

Mick snatched her out, and put her down. The bee went lazily on its way. But Daisy . . . .

Nobody had ever seen Daisy run, but now we did. Like a white streak of lightning.

Venus was next, black as a thundercloud.

'Come ON!' Mick yelled.

As we all bumped into each other the lightning streak went under the gate.

When we reached the alley there was no
Daisy. Just Mrs Thresher's open gate. And
Venus looking down at us from the top of Mrs
Thresher's fence.

Mick jumped at Venus. '*Where's my Daisy*?'

Mrs Thresher's head bobbed up.

'What are you wicked children doing chasing that poor cat? Her milk will addle, and her
kittens will die.'

We were speechless.

'Now go away and leave her in peace.'

Turning our backs on Mrs Thresher we
walked slowly back to the garden. Pat found his
voice first. 'What's "addle"?' Nobody knew.

We ran to find Mum.

'Addle means "go off",' she said.

'I once ate some fish that had gone off, and it
didn't kill me,' Pat told us. 'The kittens will just
burp a bit, that's all.'

'But *WHAT ABOUT MY DAISY?*' Mick
was frantic.

Mum went and called to Mrs Thresher over
the fence.

'Have you seen a white rabbit?'

'Certainly not.' Mrs Thresher tossed her

head. We watched it wobble on her neck. 'Only four wicked children chasing a nursing mother.'

'You did no such thing,' said Mum angrily.

'I know what I know.'

Dad came home. He sniffed at his dinner in the oven. We'd just told him about Daisy when we heard . . . .

'*Aaaarrrggghhh!*'

I knew that sound. 'It's Mr Thresher. Something's upset him.'

We ran into the garden. There was a lot of banging about next door.

'What's he doing?' Mick said. 'Is it Daisy?'

Dad stepped into his flower-bed and looked over the fence. He spoke to Mr Thresher, but he didn't answer.

Then Dad climbed right over the fence. We rushed forward, hanging on to the top. Mr Thresher still took no notice, but bashed about with a shovel. Dad dodged forward and parted some leaves.

There was Daisy gone lazy again. Dad snatched her up and handed her safely across the fence.

Mr Thresher threw down his shovel. He put his hands on his hips, and roared again.

'Sorry, old man,' Dad said when he stopped.

'Old man, is it now?' snarled Mr Thresher. 'And will being sorry bring back my lettuces? *Old man?*'

We all looked at Daisy. Fast asleep in Mick's arms, and fat as a cushion.

Dad climbed back and dug up every one of his own lettuces. He handed them over the fence to Mr Thresher.

'And what am I supposed to do with these?'

'Eat them,' Dad said, and went indoors for his dinner.

When Venus's kittens were old enough Mum wrote out new notices. WANTED: GOOD HOMES FOR KITTENS. APPLY 54 CUCKOO LANE.

This time people did. First one. Then another. And another. Until only little Pluto was left. I hoped he'd be allowed to stay, but the family the other side of the alley had a mouse, so they took him.

'Cheer up,' Dad said. 'He's gone to a good home. Probably grow as big as a tiger.'

Venus didn't mind losing her kittens in the least. Now she had all Dad's attention. The moment he sat down she jumped on his lap.

'And what . . . ' Mum said, ' . . . about *her*?'

Venus opened her eyes and looked at Dad.

'Oh, Mum. Be quiet. She understands!'

'She understands your father.'

Dad stroked Venus, who closed her eyes and purred.

'And who is going to cook her food?'

'I will, I will.'

'You won't.'

'I would,' Dad said. 'But I can't get up. I've got the cat.'

'The cat's got you. Right where she wants you. Her willing slave.'

Venus loved Dad so much she followed him everywhere. Right down to the bus stop in the mornings. When he came home she'd run to meet him and sniff his trouser legs. She could smell Bob, the eel and pie man's dog.

'She's jealous,' Mum said. 'I know exactly how she feels.'

One day Venus followed me down Cuckoo Lane.

'Go home,' I told her. But she came inside my best friend's house.

First she cleared Fred's plate. Then she captured a ball of wool, and wound it round my best friend's grandmother.

'You'll catch it,' the old lady said, 'when Fred finds you.'

But where was Fred? And where was my best friend?

Venus followed me into the garden. Past the pond, and the little hopping frogs. Right on into the jungle.

My best friend was pushing her dolls' pram along the bumpy path which ran by the side of the ditch. She didn't often play with dolls. Never in the jungle.

And there was something funny about my best friend's doll. The coat and scarf her grandmother had knitted were just as usual. The big white bonnet . . . but, oh, the face! Ginger and furry, with yellow eyes!

Then the 'doll' saw Venus.

As the pram cover rose up high in the air a hissing, spitting thing burst out. Venus took one look and ran.

The scarf, the coat and the big white bonnet came off about the jungle. We were ages finding them.

Fred never let my best friend dress him up again. Venus never followed me either. She didn't even follow Dad, but settled down to a quiet life. Just teasing Skipper from a safe distance. And visiting her growing son, Pluto, from time to time.

11
. . . and Turned a Fetching Colour

It was hot summer. No more school. By my window was a pile of little stones, one for each day until our holiday. Every morning I threw one out into the front garden.

Venus pushed into my bedroom. She jumped on my bed, and curled in my warm place next to Charlie.

'I wish you could come on holiday too.' I thought of Venus shut out in the garden. Suppose Pat and Mick forgot to feed her? Suppose she went and found another family to live with? I felt all weak and wobbly.

Dad came.

'So this is where Venus is. She knows something is going to happen. And you're very late for a Sunday morn . . . .' His mouth dropped open.

'Why are you staring at me like that?'

'Heavens above!'

When Dad had gone I wobbled to my mirror. Heavens above, indeed! *I'd turned mustard yellow!*

Mum came.

'Trust you to do it now!'

Do what? I hadn't done anything.

She sent Dad away to fetch the doctor. Then she turned Venus out, and made me get back into bed.

When Dad returned he said the doctor would come when he'd had his breakfast.

'Was he very cross?' Mum asked.

'She didn't fall ill on a Sunday on purpose.'

'Am I really ill?'

Dad patted me cautiously on the head. 'Don't you feel ill?'

'I don't know.'

Mum went and fetched soap and a flannel, a towel and a bowl of water. She gave me a good wash, but I still stayed yellow. Then she tucked me up, tight and uncomfortable, fit for a doctor to see.

When the doctor came he wasn't cross at all.

'My,' he said admiringly. 'What a fetching colour we are today.'

84

I felt better at once. 'I'm not ill, am I?'

'Sorry, old bean. You've got jaundice. I'm afraid you're in for a lonely time.'

'But I'm going to the seaside . . . .'

He shook his head.

After a bit I got up and threw out my last six stones, all together.

Mum came running up the stairs. 'Trust you! Couldn't you have waited until after the doctor had gone?'

I heard Dad laughing, but I still had to go back to bed.

When my best friend came to call I went to

my window and banged. She waved. Stared.
And her mouth dropped open . . . .

'Go back to bed at once!' Mum called.

I lay in bed and looked at Gloria. Pink and
perfect. Dangling her legs from the window of
the shoe. I picked up Charlie and threw him at
her. He flopped on the ground and one of his
ears fell off. I felt awful.

It was so hot that night I couldn't sleep. I
counted the shoe children.

Mum came with a drink of barley water.

'The old woman in the shoe has ninety-three
children,' I told her.

'One is enough for me,' Mum said. 'Now go
to sleep.'

'I can't, I can't. I've counted and counted,
and I'm still awake.'

Dad had another idea. 'Listen to the crickets
in the wall outside.'

'What crickets? What wall?'

'Just listen,' he said.

Next morning a stone hit my window.
Mick.

I was so pleased to see him I forgot about
being yellow. He looked up. Stared . . . .

People's mouths dropping was getting boring. I leaned right out of the window.

'Have a good look. Why don't you!'

But Mick rushed away in case any germs flew out and got him.

Pat came to look. He stood. Stared . . . .

'Cor! Suppose she stays like that for ever?'

Skipper came out and saw them both off, and I didn't care one bit.

But I *was* lonely. Venus wasn't allowed. Mum had sewn Charlie's ear back on, but now his stuffing was coming out. And I was fed up with Gloria.

'She's always the same,' I told Dad. 'With her ringlets and everything.'

He fetched a pencil and gave her a little beard and moustache.

'Oh, Dad! What will Mum say?'

'"Trust you",' Dad said.

And she did.

That night I listened to the crickets again. Next morning there was a basket on my floor. A basket with a rope inside, and a note.

GET REDDY FOR PARCILS

I opened the window wide and waited.

Skipper came out. He raised his leg against a tree, mooched about, and began to bark.

My best friend was coming up Cuckoo Lane. Grown-up people stop for Skipper, but my best friend walked bravely on. She came into the front garden and closed the gate behind her.

'Are you ready?' she called. 'Let down the basket.'

She dropped in a parcel. 'Now pull it up.'

Inside the parcel was a new pack of crayons.

'Thanks!'

'There's more.'

I let the empty basket fall . . . plomp!

'Mind out,' my best friend said. 'I'm not to touch what you've touched.' She dropped another parcel into the basket.

In this one was a small black woollen cat.

'My grandmother made it,' my best friend said proudly.

That wasn't the end of the basket post.

Mrs Cobley sent up a bunch of flowers. Mick put in loads of old Beanos. Pat gave me a lollipop which stuck to the bottom. Even Mr Wood, the builder, came with a book. It was called *Robinson Crusoe* and was about a man stranded on a desert island.

One day I got up extra early to stand by my basket.

Dad had read me all *Robinson Crusoe*. I knew the Beanos by heart. Mrs Cobley's flowers had wilted and died. I'd done so many drawings the crayons were broken to bits. If only I could go outside . . . .

Then I saw myself in the mirror.

I ran into Mum and Dad's bedroom.

'Look at me! *Look at me!*'

Mum groaned into her pillow.

Poor Mum. Up and down the stairs with barley water. Dad drawing on the wallpaper. No holiday by the sea.

Dad came in with her morning cup of tea.

'I'll let you into a little secret,' he told me.

'What is it? What is it?'

'You're not a fetching colour any more.'

'I know. *I know!*' I jumped on the bed and the tea shot all over.

But instead of saying 'Trust you,' Mum sat up and hugged me.

'Now I can go out,' I said.

But the house had got bigger while I'd been away. Walking downstairs felt very peculiar. The garden wall was a long way off.

I never found the crickets which lived inside. But the holes I chipped looking were just right for secret messages. My best friend and I used it all that summer. We called it the cricket post.

12

. . . and Lost a Fox Fur, and a Lot More Besides

'Next Saturday your aunts are coming to tea.'

I grinned at Mum, and she smiled at me.

The town aunts were good news. I could dress up in their clothes. Mum would have a good gossip. And we'd all enjoy a tremendous feast.

I asked if my best friend could come as well.

'As long as you're not noisy.'

'Noisy? *US?*'

I went and wrote a message and put it in the cricket post.

SATERDAY ARENTS DRESING UP

It was our favourite game just then. We'd been mothers. Grandmothers. Queens and princesses. But never aunts. And the town aunts were really fancy dressers.

Next time I looked in the wall there was

another message.

CUMING SAT GOD

I looked up at the sky, and Pat and Mick ran out of the alley and captured me.

'So that's what they do with that wall,' Mick said.

The cricket post was a secret no longer.

Pat stopped whistling through his gap. '"Cuming Sat God"?'

'"Cuming" is coming. "Sat" could be Saturday. And "God" is good,' said Mick. 'Amen.'

They both turned on me.

'What is happening on Saturday?'

I wouldn't tell them anything. My best friend and I were going to have the town aunts all to ourselves.

On Saturday afternoon we hid behind the wall to wait. We waited and waited.

'Suppose they don't come?' my best friend said.

'They're always late. They have to dress up, go to the shops, and catch the train. And the

92

Number 55 bus. They'll come.'

Later on two people turned the corner, one short, one tall.

'It's them!'

'At last.' We started out, but my best friend stopped. 'You didn't say there'd be dogs.'

'What dogs?'

'The ones they're carrying.'

'They're furs. I told you. The town aunts are fancy dressers.'

'And eaters, you said.'

'And eaters too.' I pointed to the parcels.

We started to run.

The town aunts opened their arms out wide. They kissed us, called us 'dear' and 'darling', and gave us their parcels to carry.

We made so much noise walking down Cuckoo Lane that people looked out of their windows to watch. Mrs Thresher came out and leaned on her gate. The town aunts laughed, and swept into our house.

Leaving the parcels on the kitchen table we followed them upstairs.

Mum and Dad's bed was soon covered with coats. Hats. Gloves. Furs. The town aunts

93

kicked off their high-heeled shoes. They patted their hair, and powdered their noses. The room was full of a lovely scent.

Then down we all went to open the parcels.

There were chocolate fingers. Coconut cream. Brandy snaps. An iced cake and walnut whips.

Mum made tea in her best silver pot. The best china stood ready on the best silver tray. There were cucumber sandwiches, sausage rolls, and a Dundee cake, as well as everything else.

We packed our share of the feast in the cake box. When Mum and the aunts were safely shut up we crept back upstairs to the bedroom.

'What shall we do first?' my best friend said. 'Eat or dress up?'

'Dress up.'

My best friend wasn't sure.

'Then we can have a whopping big feast afterwards. And eat the whole lot in one go.'

I put on my tall aunt's mauve silk coat. Her black straw hat. And the high-heeled shoes.

'You do look funny,' my best friend said. 'Miss Baloni gone barmy.'

I didn't want to look like Miss Baloni, but my glamorous, exciting town aunt.

My best friend disappeared inside my short aunt's coat. She pulled on a hat like a chimney pot.

'*You* look like Green Hill.'

My best friend snatched up a chocolate finger.

'Not yet!'

'Why not?'

And that's when it all went wrong.

As I tottered forward to grab the cake box a

cucumber sandwich flew out. My best friend trod on it and fell over. Clutching at the bed she pulled off a fox fur.

'Eurgh! I don't like it. Take it away!'

Instead I wriggled the fox fur towards her.

She climbed on to the dressing table. I threw the fur, and she threw it back. It hit the window, and flopped on the ledge.

Outside somebody whistled.

'Did you see that?'

'It's not a cat.'

'Nor a dog.'

'Nor a rabbit.'

'It's a fox!'

My best friend climbed down. We crawled beneath the window. I reached up and wriggled the fox. And giggled. And wriggled. And the more I did the more I couldn't stop. And my best friend couldn't either. Until . . . .

The fur fell out of the window.

We got tangled up in the town aunts' coats. By the time we looked out Pat and Mick were in the alley, and the fox fur with them.

Downstairs a door opened. Shrieks of laughter blew up the stairs. Then Mum called.

'Are you two still up there?'

'Yes.'

'You're not to touch your aunts' things with your sticky fingers.'

If only that was all we had done!

'Go out into the garden.'

We laid the clothes back on the bed. Took the cake box, and ran downstairs.

Pat and Mick were in the alley, stroking the fox.

'Poor thing,' said Mick fiercely. 'How would you like it? Glass beads for eyes. Your insides out, and lined with silk.'

'It's not my fault,' I said.

'We'll bury it. That's what we'll do. Deep in the jungle, where nobody will ever find it.' Pat began whistling.

'You can't!' I said.

They walked away.

'I must have it back. I must, I must. I'll give you . . . .'

'What?'

They stood at the top of the alley and waited.

I held out the box. ' . . . some of this.'

They took the whole lot, and ran off with it.

After we'd put the fox fur back we went to see how far Mum and the town aunts had got with their tea. All that talking and laughing.... There couldn't have been much time for eating.

But....

My best friend stared, and so did I. The best china plates were covered in crumbs, nothing else!

As we walked to the bus stop with the town aunts Mrs Thresher leaned on her gate to watch. Windows opened. The fox furs bounced on the town aunts' chests.

'Did you have a lovely feed, my darlings?'

We couldn't speak, just nodded instead. And tried not to think about sausage rolls. Coconut cream. Brandy snaps. Walnut whips. Iced cake. Chocolate fingers. Even a cucumber sandwich would have been something.

As they kissed us goodbye the air was full of their lovely scent. We waved goodbye, then walked back slowly.

'The rotten things,' my best friend said. 'The greedy, rotten things.'

We nearly missed the message in the cricket post.

98

LOCK IN PIT

'What "lock"?'

'Perhaps it's "look",' my best friend said. 'But what is "pit"?'

'"Pit" *is* pit.'

We rushed down the garden. On top of the old dead summer flowers sat the cake box. Inside were two walnuts. Some broken bits of brandy snap. A coconut cream stuck up with cucumber slices. And half a sausage roll.

'They're not all rotten,' I said. 'Well, not quite.'

13
. . . and Went on the Wide Dark Ocean

'I do not want to hear of any accidents.'

Miss Baloni's eyes bored into us. Assembly had gone on and on. And it wasn't over yet.

'No playing with matches, or fireworks. Watch out for bonfires. Keep pets indoors safe. And TAKE GOOD CARE.' Miss Baloni paused, but only to draw breath.

'What must you do?'

'TAKE GOOD CARE, MISS BALONI.'

At playtime we exploded into the playground.

There was to be a big bonfire in the middle of the jungle. My best friend's father was taking her. Mick was going too. Dad was bringing fireworks home to let off in our garden.

Only Pat was broody. Mr Cross had a dent in his head from playing with fireworks when he was a boy. Pat would be shut up safe indoors on Guy Fawkes night.

All through the day of November the Fifth we chattered. Fidgeted. And waited.

When the sky grew dark it began. A few little pops. Then swishes and bangs. Distant snatches of voices. A haze round the street lamps down Cuckoo Lane. And a creeping, strange, exciting smell.

A shape loomed up. Dad at last, with a parcel under one arm.

'Where's Venus?' he asked.

'On my bed safe, with Charlie and the little black cat.'

I took the parcel into the kitchen. Inside was a box. And inside that . . . .

Fat sticks. Thin sticks. Short and long sticks. Cones and wrigglies. All done up in purple packets.

As I lifted out the rockets Mum looked in the oven.

'Dinner?' she asked Dad. 'Or get this over and done with first?'

Over and done with!

Dad told her to shut the oven door, and sent me to fetch his old gardening coat.

First he pinned Catherine Wheels on the

trellis. They caught and spun, blue, green and crimson. Sometimes they stuck, and Dad gave them a push.

In the middle of the garden he put a bucket of sand for the cones and sticks to stand in. Golden Rain and Silver Fountains. Roman Candles. Fiery Dragons. Mount Everest. One by one they lived, and died.

Dad flung away the jumping squibs. When they came jumping back we rushed indoors.

Then we ran out again for the rockets. WHOOSH!

Pink and yellow balls of light dropped from the sky like giant bubbles. And as they dropped I saw . . . a white ghost face and hands.

WHOOSH!

The third rocket flew.

WHOOSH!

And still the ghost was there, pressed against the Crosses' window.

The family the other side of the alley had a bonfire. Sparks big as puddings were in the air.

'Dad! Look out!'

A spark had dropped. The last rocket fired. TOO SOON! It tore towards the bottom fence. Over the top, then straight for the Crosses'. The ghost disappeared, and the rocket crashed on the roof above.

'That's that over and done with,' Mum said.

But it wasn't.

In the firework box there was still another packet.

'Sparklers,' Dad said. 'Those are safe to light indoors.'

But somebody was knocking on our front door. I ran to open it and there was Mrs Cobley.

'There's such a sight out in the jungle. All wasted on an old woman like me.'

'You mean . . . . I can come and watch?'

Mrs Cobley nodded. 'There's a grand view from my upstairs window.' She nodded at Mum and Dad. 'She'll be quite safe.'

'What about Skipper?' Dad asked.

'Under the table, with his head in his paws. He'll not come out until it's all over.'

As I put my sparklers in my pocket I remembered the ghost.

'Please, can Pat come too?'

'As long as he doesn't run off,' Mrs Cross said when we knocked on her door.

'Don't worry,' said Mrs Cobley. 'He'll go no further than my upstairs room.'

All the same she kept a tight hold on Pat as we walked through the alley, across Cuckoo Lane and into her house.

The upstairs room was full of junk. Boxes and cases. A broken dog basket. Old cushions and lampshades. A sea captain's hat.

Pat put on the captain's hat, and I put on a lampshade.

We turned off the light and looked out of

the window.

'We're crossing a wide black ocean,' Pat said.

'What's that, in the middle?'

'An island with a burning volcano.'

'Is it dangerous?'

'Oh yes, it's dangerous all right. Our engines have stopped. If we're swept ashore we'll probably be killed.'

'I don't want to be killed.'

'Give me a sparkler then.' The captain hurried below. When he came back the sparkler was lit. 'That's one engine firing. Now light another one off the end.'

We lit four.

'Full Steam Ahead!' the captain said.

We sailed across the wide black ocean, and before the sparklers could fizzle out we lit some more.

As the volcano burned lower a screamer tore across the sky.

'That's the Roaring Forties,' Pat said. 'A great big wind that blows over the Southern Oceans.'

'How do you know?'

'My dad told me. Soon we'll be near the South Pole. Then there'll be pack ice.'

Something sharp hit the window.

'See?' said the captain.

Water ran down before our eyes. The volcano went out. The ocean was covered with little bobbing lights. Then it was just dark, and wet.

'We're there.'

'Where?'

'Australia, I think.' Pat took off the captain's hat, and dropped it next to the burnt-out sparklers. 'You do look barmy in that lampshade.'

We went downstairs.

Mrs Cobley gave us cocoa and hot pasties. Pat looked at all the pictures on the walls, and saw the ship in the bottle. And afterwards we listened to stories about Captain Cobley.

When Skipper came out from under the table we went home.

As we ran across the road Pat said, 'One day, when I'm captain of a real ship, I shall sail right round the world.'

I wonder if he did.

Other Titles in Andersen Young Readers' Library

Roger Collinson

Get Lavinia Goodbody!
Paper Flags and Penny Ices

Philip Curtis

A Gift from Another Galaxy
A Party for Lester
Bewitched by the Brain Sharpeners
Chaos Comes to Chivvy Chase
Mr Browser and the Brain Sharpeners
Mr Browser and the Comet Crisis
Mr Browser and the Mini-Meteorites
Mr Browser in the Space Museum
The Brain Sharpeners Abroad
The Quest of the Quidnuncs
The Revenge of the Brain Sharpeners

Elfie Donnelly

Odd Stockings

Christopher Hein

Jamie and His Friends

Nigel Hinton

Run to Beaver Towers

Julia Jarman

Ollie and the Bogle
Poppy and the Vicarage Ghost
When Poppy Ran Away

Pat McAughey

Lost Emerald

Christine Nostlinger

Conrad
Mr Bat's Great Invention

John Singleton

The Adventures of Muckpup

Brenda Sivers

Biminy in Danger